Donald Trump is a White Supremacist, Tax Dodger, and Russian Spy

THE EVIDENCE

I0408073

HARVEY VOLSON

"All of the women on 'The Apprentice' flirted with me — consciously or unconsciously. That's to be expected."

-Donald Trump

Table of Contents

(By having Hillary Clinton use a private e-mail server that got hacked by the Russians)

MAKING TROLLING GREAT AGAIN

CHAPTER 1

DONALD TRUMP IS A WHITE SUPREMACIST

Shocking Evidence

Nothing here, try the next page

MAKING EVIDENCE GREAT AGAIN

Trump train

Who needs evidence when you have fake news?

DONALD TRUMP IS PRESIDENT

DONALD TRUMP IS YOUR PRESIDENT

NO EVIDENCE OF WHITE SUPREMACY HERE

ALL GOOD

NO EVIDENCE PROVIDED

FAKE NEWS

TRUMP

DEPLORABLE ARMY

THE EVIDENCE

THE EVIDENCE

THE EVIDENCE

THE EVIDENCE

THE EVIDENCE

Nothing here, try the next page

Nothing here, try the next page

Nothing here, try the next page

giggitty

Chapter 2

Donald Trump is a Tax Dodger

Chapter 2
Donald Trump is a Tax Dodger

NO REAL EVIDENCE

NO REAL EVIDENCE

DETAILED EVIDENCE COMING NEVER

NO REAL EVIDENCE

TAXATION IS THEFT

NO REAL EVIDENCE

NO REAL EVIDENCE

NO REAL EVIDENCE

NO REAL EVIDENCE

FAKE NEWS

FAKE NEWS

FAKE NEWS

TAXATION IS THEFT

TAXATION IS THEFT

TAXATION IS THEFT

TAXATION IS THEFT

TAXATION IS THEFT

FAKE NEWS

FAKE NEWS

FAKE NEWS

FAKE NEWS

FAKE NEWS

FAKE NEWS

FAKE NEWS

FAKE NEWS

FAKE NEWS!!

Chapter 3

Donald Trump is a Russian Spy

Donald Trump is a Russian Spy

MORE FAKE NEWS!!

MORE FAKE NEWS!!

MORE FAKE NEWS!!

MORE FAKE NEWS!!

MORE FAKE NEWS!!

MORE FAKE NEWS!!

MORE FAKE NEWS!!

MORE FAKE NEWS!!

MORE FAKE NEWS!!

giggitty

Chapter 4

Donald Trump Rigged the Elections

Donald Trump Rigged the Elections

Chapter 4

Donald Trump Rigged the Elections

Chapter 4

Donald Trump Rigged the Elections

Donald Trump Rigged the Elections

Donald Trump Rigged the Elections

Donald Trump Rigged the Elections

Chapter 4

Donald Trump Rigged the Elections

Chapter 4

Donald Trump Rigged the Elections

Chapter 4

Donald Trump Rigged the Elections

Chapter 4

Donald Trump Rigged the Elections

giggitty

giggitty

giggitty

giggitty

GIGGITTY!!

GIGGITTY

GIGGITTY

GIGGITTY

GIGGITTY

GIGGITTY

GIGGITTY

GIGGITTY

GIGGITTY

GIGGITTY

GIGGITTY

GIGGITTY

GIGGITTY

GIGGITTY

GIGGITTY

GIGGITTY

GIGGITTY

HEY HO

Bibliography

Fake News

Fake News

Fake News

Fake News

Fake News

Fake News

Fake News

Did you find the evidence persuasive?